Skomer

Portrait of a Welsh island

GRAFFEG

Published by Graffeg
First published 2007
Copyright © Graffeg 2007
ISBN 978-1905582-08-2

Graffeg, Radnor Court, 256 Cowbridge Road
East, Cardiff CF5 1GZ Wales UK.
Tel: +44(0)29 2037 7312
sales@graffeg.com www.graffeg.com
Graffeg are hereby identified as the authors
of this work in accordance with section 77
of the Copyrights, Designs and Patents
Act 1988.

Distributed by the Welsh Books Council
www.cllc.org.uk
castellbrychan@cllc.org.uk

A CIP Catalogue record for this book is
available from the British Library.

Designed and produced by
Peter Gill & Associates
sales@petergill.com
www.petergill.com

Map base information reproduced by
permission of Ordnance Survey on behalf
of HMSO © Crown Copyright (2005).
All rights reserved. Ordnance Survey
Licence number 100020518

Skomer Portrait of a Welsh island
Written by Jane Matthews
with contributions from Iolo Williams
and Matthew Parris.

The publishers are also grateful to the
Welsh Books Council for their financial
support and marketing advice.
www.gwales.com

The author and publisher wish to thank all
photographers and writers who kindly
contributed to this book.
Further information on the contributors is
available on pages 154 – 157.

Every effort has been made to ensure
that the information in this book is current
and it is given in good faith at the time
of publication. Please be aware that
circumstances can change and be sure to
check details before making travel plans.

Skomer

Portrait of a Welsh island

GRAFFEG

Foreword

Iolo Williams

If I were to choose one Welsh nature reserve that could hold its own against any other reserve, anywhere in the world, it would have to be Skomer.

It is the diamond in the crown jewels of Welsh wildlife and little wonder, therefore, that it attracts thousands of visitors each year.

It holds a third of the world population of Manx Shearwaters, thousands of Puffins, Guillemots and Razorbills, a significant proportion of the Welsh population of Short-eared Owls, the unique Skomer Vole and the seas surrounding the island are amongst the richest in Britain.

There is no doubt that it is a naturalist's paradise and I have been privileged to visit the island on more than 40 occasions over the past 25 years. However, it is not just the wildlife that makes Skomer such a magical place.

The people, too, are very special. I have had the pleasure of walking with a succession of enthusiastic, dedicated and knowledgeable wardens and researchers, learning new facts every single time I go. Their warmth and willingness to help has always made a visit to Skomer that little bit more special.

Left: Tom's House
South-east from Skomer Head lies Tom's House and The Amos, with The Wick beyond.
Photo Dave Boyle

For anyone who has never visited the island in spring and summer, I would urge you to get out there as soon as you can. It's a unique experience, and one that will remain vivid in the memory for years afterwards.

Contents

Left: **South Haven in
the Mist**
Photo Jane Matthews

Jane Matthews

Introduction

Skomer Island lies less than a mile off shore from the Marloes Peninsula in Pembrokeshire, yet it is this short span of water that sets the island a world apart from its neighbours.

Free from all land-based predators, Skomer has evolved as its own bustling ecosystem in a unique and spectacular landscape. Covering over 300 hectares this treeless island is world famous for its breeding colonies of seabirds.

More than 6,000 pairs of Puffins nest on the cliff-tops; the largest colony in southern Britain, and they can be seen at close quarters throughout June and July fluttering in with beaks full of fish for their chicks. The island also boasts over 128,000 pairs of the Manx Shearwaters; a curious bird that only returns to land under the cloak of darkness. Its raucous call was thought by sailors to be the cries of lost souls at sea and provides a unique soundtrack to a night on the island. With thousands of shearwaters literally dropping in from the night sky during their long nesting season, the island is transformed into a strange and mystical world; the stuff of fantasy.

Many other rare and dazzling species of fauna and flora abound on Skomer and as the seasons wheel, so too revolve its colours, smells and sounds. From the psychedelic purple of the Bluebell blanket that quivers over the island in late May to the russet-red of the autumn Bracken. From whirring Guillemots to cronking Ravens, Skomer is an exotic bazaar of the natural world.

Weaved into this wilderness is man's presence on the island. Settlement remains date back to the Iron Age, giving the island its status as one of the best preserved Scheduled Ancient Monuments in Britain. Shadows of a more recent farming history lie at the centre of the island where the farm buildings still stand. The imposing ruined farmhouse is a sober relic of the harsh – but periodically prosperous – time for the island's farming population that extended through to the mid twentieth century.

Skomer is now a National Nature Reserve, owned by the Countryside Council for Wales and managed by the Wildlife Trust of South and West Wales. A small team of staff, researchers and volunteers populate the island from March to November each year, living in tune with the island and its resources. There is no mains water or mains electricity, no landlines, shops or cars. Living on Skomer is a story in itself, and one best told through the images and anecdotes of those who care most passionately for it.

Left: **Looking East from the Mainland** From Marloes Sands and the small island of Gateholm, the finger of the mainland peninsula points west to Middleholm and Skomer beyond.
Photo Andy Davies

"...See my child, how remarkable
is the Island of Skomer!
Come with me, I will show you
every cranny of its outer shore".
Hilaire Belloc, *The Cruise of
the Nona* (1925).

Left: **Skomer and Middleholm** 'Skomer' derives from 'Skalmey', the Viking name for the island: Skalm (meaning short sword, reflecting the island's shape) and ey (island). Vikings invaded the Welsh coast in 850 AD.
Photo Andy Davies

Left: **South Haven and The Neck** Erosion of softer sedimentary rock has created a narrow isthmus separating the main island from The Neck to the east.
Photo Andy Davies

The Wildlife Trust of South and West Wales

The Wildlife Trust of South and West Wales is a charitable organisation that manages 92 nature reserves, from Cardiff and Caerphilly in the east of Wales to Ceredigion and Pembrokeshire in the west, including four of the west Wales islands. These nature reserves form a land holding equal to approximately 4,000 acres; 10 lie within Special Areas of Conservation and Special Protection Areas; seven are National Nature Reserves (NNRs); 40 are Sites of Special Scientific Interest (SSSIs) and five are Scheduled Ancient Monuments.

Whilst many of the reserves are located within some of the most rural areas of the country, a proportion are found within the heart of industrial Wales and some are located within, or close to, severely deprived inner city areas. In addition to Skomer Island, the Trust manages St. Margaret's and Cardigan Islands and now owns and manages Skokholm, the island two miles south of Skomer. The Trust's work is carried out by a team of both permanent and seasonal staff, who in turn rely on dedicated groups of volunteers without whom this work would be difficult to deliver.

The Wildlife Trust of South and West Wales is one of 47 local Wildlife Trusts that, combined, manage 2,200 reserves across the whole of the UK. With 670,000 members it is the largest UK voluntary organisation dedicated to conserving a diverse range of natural habitats and species, fostering sustainable living and inspiring a love of the natural world.

For more information and educational resources please visit www.welshwildlife.org

Left: **Razorbill**
(Alca torda)
Razorbills nest on Skomer in internationally important numbers. Photo Dave Boyle

Matthew Parris

Flying hopefully into the night, leaving our cares behind.

A PALE HALF MOON was up, which was a pity. Far below we could hear a gentle Atlantic swell licking the rocks. From a cave at the cliffs' feet came the bark of a cow seal guarding her pup. The Pembrokeshire coast glimmered across a strait silvered by moonlight. The slightest of breezes stirred the Bracken...

...The reason it was a pity about the moon was that a fledgling Manx Shearwater prefers pitch black before he ventures out. Until now he has lived almost without light. Below ground in his burrow his parents' single egg was laid, guarded and incubated for nearly two months before he hatched; since then he has spent ten weeks growing fat and fluffy in the dark.

His only intimation of a world beyond the burrow has been the rush of wings outside as father or mother fly in – always at night, the darker and stormier the better – with gurgling, cackling shrieks and a delivery of liquid fish paste.

He cannot walk. He cannot fly. Of sun and sunshine he knows nothing, save that on some strange unconscious level in his tiny brain, danger and light are associated – sunlight in which his and his parents' merciless predator, the Great Black-backed Gull, can spot and target a defenceless, feathered fluffball flapping and stumbling in the Skomer Bracken. Even the weak beam of my torch now disconcerts him.

And on that same unconscious level he knows something else; that very soon – perhaps tomorrow – he must fly to Brazil. Tonight he must learn to fly.

The Manx Shearwater is one of the wonders of the world... about half of the world's entire population of this diminished but now stable species breeds on tiny Skomer (about a mile wide) and the even tinier island of Skokholm nearby.

Since rats drove shearwaters from the Calf of Man, "Manx" has become a misnomer. Everything about this bird confuses. Sailors mistook the adults' night cry – like a demented chicken's – for the screams of souls in torment. Some fool dubbed the bird a puffin, which it never was, and to this day its Latin name, *Puffinus puffinus*, bewilders students, while the French still call it the English Puffin. Until relatively recently its migrations – like its part-subterranean lifestyle – have been wrapped in mystery.

No newcomer to the species would guess that the chick – swollen by a diet of oily baby food into a big, fluff-upholstered butterball, outweighing its parents – is even related to the slim-winged, black-and-white flying ace of the Atlantic, streaking across the oceans in search of sardines to disgorge into the open beak waiting back in the burrow. Over a life of up to half a century one bird may fly further than to the Moon and back.

Above: **Pole Star** On a clear night above the Trig Point the stars are captured, in a long exposure photograph, revolving around the Pole Star. It is this night sky which is thought to form the basis of the shearwater's spectacular navigational system that leads them on their migratory passage to and from South America.
Photo Brian Hewitt

I am learning such things. With me on Skomer to help to teach
was the permanent warden stationed there by the Wildlife Trust
of South and West Wales, Juan Brown. We tied up at the jetty
after lunch. Juan directed us to the ruins of an old farm... There
are no roads or cars and we walked a grassy track through rocks
and Bracken, carrying sleeping bags... and food. A few gulls
patrolled. Rabbits gambolled. All was quiet and sunny. Nothing –
nothing except the honeycomb of burrows everywhere you looked,
and the occasional heap of feathers around a gull-pecked
fledgling corpse - alerted the rambler to a parallel universe
beneath our boots. Inches underground lay a nursery city, the
Rome of the shearwater world. Tens of thousands of hearts were
beating down there, hundreds of thousands of small hopefuls,
new-feathered, were awaiting their big moment. Their big
moment was soon.

Left: **Manx Shearwater (Puffinus puffinus), Fledgling.** With legs set so far back on their bodies shearwaters must launch themselves from the highest possible point for the best chance of take-off. The first time they get airborne will mark the start of their 7000 mile journey to South America.
Photo Mike Alexander

At dusk my producer and I walked the half-mile across to the warden's cottage, to interview him. Juan Brown knew his stuff and sounded keen, though he must have heard the questions a thousand times. I asked how fledglings know September is the time to come out of their burrows by night and learn to fly?

Their parents simply leave, he said. They fly off to South America. They just have. A few days later the chicks scramble from their burrows. Nobody is sure why.

How, I asked, do they young birds know the way to South America? Nobody is sure of that, either. Some think the bird's brain responds the Earth's magnetic field, but the great ornithologist Ronald Lockley, who lived and worked on nearby Skokholm more than 60 years ago, proved that shearwaters orient themselves best when the sky (night or day) is clear. He had two shearwaters crated up and sent to Boston in America. They arrived back in their Skokholm burrows – their exact burrows – before the letter advising of their release. How, he asked, did they do this?

Go into the night on a starry night. There is only one place on Earth from which, at (say) midnight on Tuesday, September 16, a clear sky at night will appear as it does from where you are standing – and that is where you now are. If you always knew the date and time, and if you could access a complete set of star-maps for every time and place, then you could locate yourself by selecting the map which matched the sky you see. This, it is thought, is what migrating birds may do.

But this navigational system must be pegged to a point of reference: the burrow from which the young bird first emerges – and to which, after six years feeding and maturing – he will return to breed. So, stumbling and staring around outside his front door, he is locking onto the sky. For the rest of his life all flight-paths will lead from and to this point, this starry map above one tiny hole in the surface of one tiny island in one tiny corner of the great Atlantic Ocean.

"Follow me," said Juan Brown, "now it's dark, and we'll walk up to the best area for burrows."

Something had happened to the footpath we had walked down at twilight. It was littered with baby shearwaters. You would at first have thought these birds were dying – sick, perhaps, or poisoned. Each was flopping desperately around. They could not stand; when they tried walking they would fall forward onto their breasts. Their legs were too far back to balance so they kept toppling, beak-in-the-dust.

"Having their legs set back," said Juan, "is the perfect design for pursuing fish underwater."

We reached the top of the knoll. I tried switching off our torch. It took time for my eyes to adjust to the dark. When they did, the sight was amazing. It was as if the undergrowth had come alive with pigeon-sized, two-tone, black-and-white fledglings. A few still had patches of butterball down but most had lost it.

Spreading out their wings – long, black, slim, curved and beautiful – they tried to balance. Some were crawling up rocks, cheeping, beating their wings to give them lift, clawing with webbed feet at the rock, teetering on the top, then taking off for exploratory flights which always ended in a painful and undignified crash into the Bracken.

"But they'll learn fast," said Juan, as one more advanced than his peers whirred a full 20 yards down the hill, then came a cropper.

Two chicks were necking affectionately. For all those months underground each may have thought himself the only chick in the world, alone but for the parental beak with its fishpaste meal.

"They mate for life," said Juan.

Everywhere you looked, dark shapes floundered around. On every rock a teetering chick clambered for possession and a launch pad. The whole island, to every horizon, was alive with them. We stood and wondered for an hour.

"You should have been here before the parents left," said Juan. "The noise is amazing".

He explained that on arrival from South America the breeding pairs float just offshore in great rafts of birds, waiting until nightfall. Then, under the cover of the dark, they dive straight in, each for precisely the nest from which they came.

When the egg is laid the parents take it in turns to incubate, and later to fetch food. But they come in only at night – the darker and stormier the better – shrieking to their chick, from whom they always seem to be able to identify from the thousands of others.

Returning to our cabin around midnight I slept peacefully but awoke in the small hours and hearing flapping, walked out into the dark.

All the stars were out. The Milky Way was clear and strong. I stood there alone for a long time. Apart from the apprentice flyers clawing, crashing and flip-flopping in every direction, I was alone beneath a vast sky. A cold breeze hinted at an approaching autumn. As I stood, a young shearwater lurched over my foot – then began to climb my leg, his wings beating. To him I suppose I was just another rock.

What did he know of the journey which lay ahead? He may still be on his travels when mine are over.

I felt as I stood there a solitary and privileged witness to a supremely important moment in the life not only of individuals but of a species. Beneath the canopy of the stars, something immense and timeless was stirring...

Skomer island

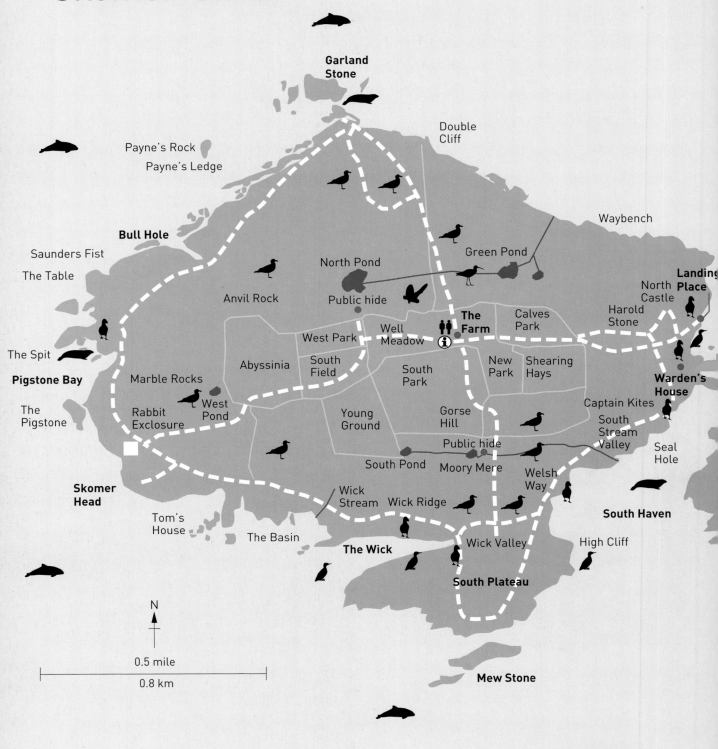

Garland Stone

Double Cliff

Payne's Rock

Payne's Ledge

Waybench

Bull Hole

Green Pond

Saunders Fist

The Table

North Pond

Landing Place

North Castle

Anvil Rock

Public hide

Harold Stone

The Spit

Well Meadow

The Farm

Calves Park

Pigstone Bay

West Park

Warden's House

The Pigstone

Abyssinia

South Field

South Park

New Park

Shearing Hays

Captain Kites

Marble Rocks

West Pond

Rabbit Exclosure

Young Ground

Gorse Hill

South Stream Valley

Seal Hole

Skomer Head

Public hide

South Pond

Moory Mere

Welsh Way

South Haven

Tom's House

Wick Stream

Wick Ridge

Wick Valley

High Cliff

The Basin

The Wick

South Plateau

Mew Stone

N

0.5 mile

0.8 km

Broad Sound

Key

- - - Trails
- 🚹🚺ℹ️ Toilets & Information
- Curlews
- Puffin colonies
- Cliff nesting seabirds
- Gull colonies
- Short-eared Owls
- Grey Seals
- Porpoises

St Brides Bay

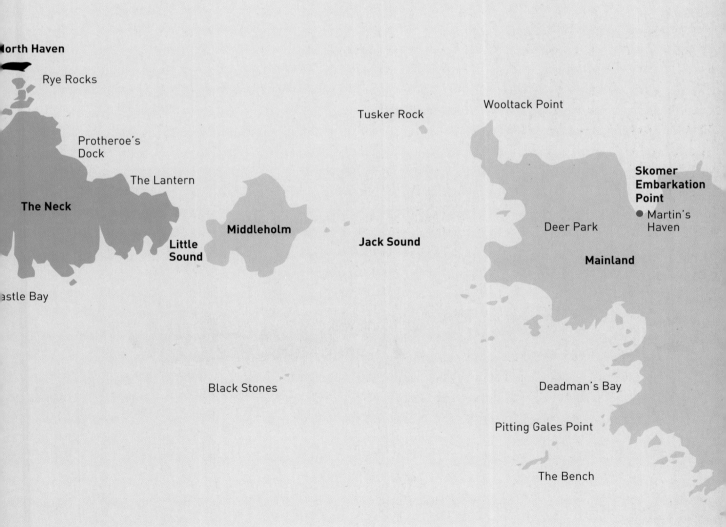

North Haven

Rye Rocks

Tusker Rock

Wooltack Point

Protheroe's Dock

The Lantern

Skomer Embarkation Point

● Martin's Haven

The Neck

Middleholm

Deer Park

Little Sound

Jack Sound

Mainland

Castle Bay

Black Stones

Deadman's Bay

Pitting Gales Point

The Bench

Seasonal timeline

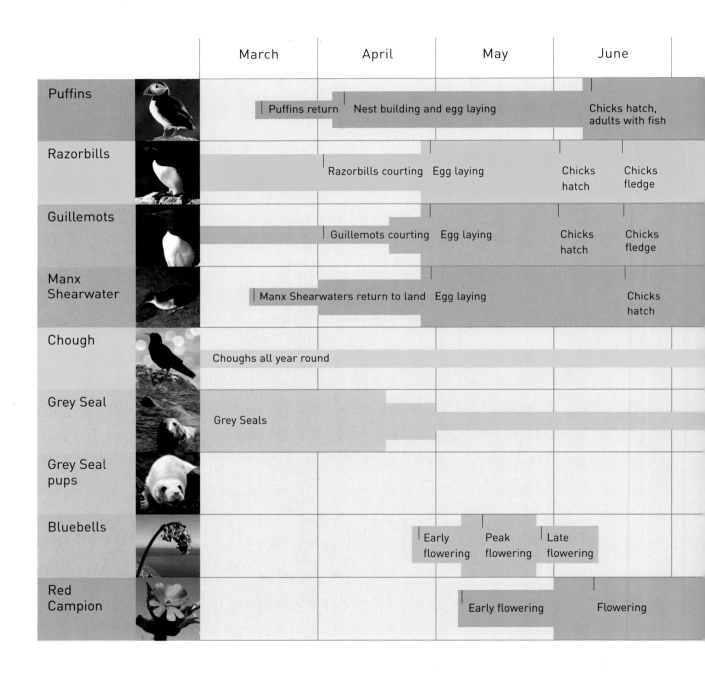

		March	April	May	June
Puffins		Puffins return	Nest building and egg laying		Chicks hatch, adults with fish
Razorbills			Razorbills courting Egg laying		Chicks hatch Chicks fledge
Guillemots			Guillemots courting Egg laying		Chicks hatch Chicks fledge
Manx Shearwater		Manx Shearwaters return to land Egg laying			Chicks hatch
Chough		Choughs all year round			
Grey Seal		Grey Seals			
Grey Seal pups					
Bluebells				Early flowering Peak flowering Late flowering	
Red Campion				Early flowering	Flowering

Skomer Island is open to the public:
April to October.

July	August	September	October	November

Chicks fledge | Adults leave

Adults leave
Fledglings exercise then leave

Early pups | Grey Seal pups

Water

Since 1990 the waters around Skomer have been protected and currently constitute one of only three Marine Nature Reserves in the UK. The warm flow of the Gulf Stream mixes with colder northern waters to create this rich marine environment. Surrounded by such a lavish food source, and protected from predators like the fox, rat and weasel, the island's bird populations can thrive.

Above right: **Jack Sound** Looking east from the mainland across the Sound towards Middleholm, and Skomer beyond. Even on calm days its currents and eddies can be deceptively strong.
Photo Andy Davies

Right: **Prince** Skomer's last working horse, Prince, is pictured with Reuben Codd who farmed the island in the thirties and forties, before the island became a Nature Reserve in 1959
Photo Roscoe Howells

Jack Sound runs fast and furious between Skomer and the mainland and has at times, throughout the ages, been a perilous hazard to man and beast. When Skomer was a farmstead animals were sometimes brought to the island under their own steam – literally – as cattle and horses were made to swim through the tumbling channel. Prince, Skomer's last working horse who swam the sound in 1947, was said to have been so distressed by his passage that he never again ventured as far as the landing point at North Haven and refused to return to the mainland in retirement. In 1967 the ship The Lucy, laden with carbide, hit rocks in the Sound and came to rest on the sea-bed forty metres down at the entrance to North Haven. The wreck is now one of Britain's most spectacular dive sites.

Above: **Boarding the Dale Princess**
Left: **Crossing**
Right: **Approaching Skomer** The crossing from Martin's Haven to Skomer takes just 15 minutes and provides the ideal opportunity, at the right time of year, to spot porpoises, seabirds and seals along the way.
Photos Andy Davies, Jane Matthews, Richard Brown

From April to October **the Dale Princess** sails to the island bringing visitors and supplies. Up to 250 people can land each day that the island is open. However by late September weather fronts and rough seas can severely restrict the crossings. Islanders remain at the mercy of the waves and can be marooned for weeks at a time.

The open arms of North Haven form the gateway to this offshore wilderness. Managing the island requires a fine balance; allowing public access without compromising the very wildlife which makes it so special.

Left: **Visitors Landing on Skomer** A steep bank of steps greets the visitor to Skomer but, once at the top, the island's plateau is gentle and the walk is relatively easy. A route around the island takes approximately three hours, at a leisurely pace.
Photo Jeff Morgan

Above: **Skipper** Kenny Gainfort has been skippering the Dale Princess for over 15 years.
Photo Jane Matthews

Left: **Gutting Mackerel**
A quiet moment on the Dale Princess gives co-skipper Karl Wonnacott time to prepare his dinner.
Photo Bob Ball

Right: **Feeding Frenzy**
Over 30,000 pairs of Gannets breed on Grassholm, seven miles west of Skomer. A large bird with black wing-tips and a yellow-buff head, the Gannet can be seen plunge-diving for fish, often amongst feeding porpoises. Seen here with Manx Shearwaters out at sea during the day.
Photo Lyndon Lomax

Seabirds reign over these grey-green waters, wholly dependent on the ecosystems within.

Above: **Fulmar (Fulmaris glacialis)**
Skomer's population of Fulmars rose from just four pairs in 1960 to over 700 pairs in the nineties, as part of a southerly spread of the species throughout the British Isles.
Photo Dave Boyle

The protection and study of this fragile ecology is essential. **Future changes** in sea temperature could have a dramatic effect on the health of these waters and every species it supports.

Above: **MNR boat**
Middle: **Dive Preparation**
Photos Blaise Bullimore (MNR)
Below: **Going Down**
Photo Andy Davies
As well as education and the protection of the coastal environment, the work of the Marine Nature Reserve staff involves many hours of close monitoring below sea level.

Above: **North Haven**
Dense kelp forests waft
in the swell of the
shallower waters in
North Haven.
Photo David Miller

After Pembrokeshire's disastrous *Sea Empress* oil spill of 1995 **recovery of the ecosystems** above and below the waves has been meticulously monitored by Marine Nature Reserve staff.

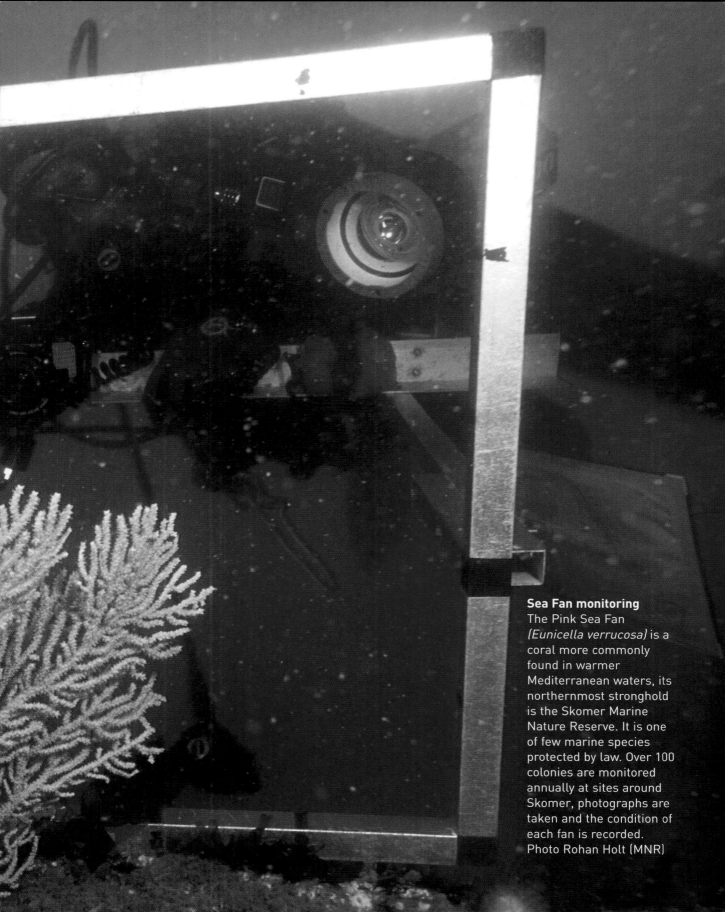

Sea Fan monitoring
The Pink Sea Fan
(*Eunicella verrucosa*) is a
coral more commonly
found in warmer
Mediterranean waters, its
northernmost stronghold
is the Skomer Marine
Nature Reserve. It is one
of few marine species
protected by law. Over 100
colonies are monitored
annually at sites around
Skomer, photographs are
taken and the condition of
each fan is recorded.
Photo Rohan Holt (MNR)

Superbly camouflaged, this rare sea slug has only been recorded in the Reserve on two occasions.

Sea Fan Nudibranchs
(*Tritonia nilsodherni*)
Nudibranchs are commonly known as sea slugs. They are all carnivores and most have a very selective choice of food. This nudibranch feeds only on the Pink Sea Fan and has evolved to perfectly mimic its polyps.
Photo Mark Burton (MNR)

Free floating plankton are paralysed by the stinging tentacles of jellyfish, passed to the mouth and then digested in the central stomach.

Compass Jellyfish
(Chrysaora hysoscella)
These majestic creatures can be found throughout the Reserve in the summer months.
Photo Rob Gibbs (MNR)

Around The Mew Stone deep gullies are found below the sea surface. Water is forced through them in strong surges and only marine life with a good hold will survive.

Left: **Gooseberry Sea Squirts** *(Dendrodoa grossularia)*
The Gooseberry Sea Squirt thrives in this turbulent undersea environment forming large carpets on the rocks and filtering the plankton-rich water. Photo Blaise Bullimore (MNR)

Above: **Crayfish** *(Palinurus elegans)*
Crayfish and lobsters are predators on the rocky reefs. Commercial fishing for crustaceans continues despite a recent campaign to abolish all fishing in the waters surrounding the island. Photo Kate Lock (MNR)

Left: **Dahlia Anemone
(Urticina felina)**
Flower-like anemones
are actually predators
equipped with stinging
tentacles ready to
capture food. Anemones
come in many forms,
sizes and colour; 40
species have been
recorded in the Reserve.
Photo Blaise Bullimore
(MNR)

Below left: **Serrated
Wrack (Fucus serratus)**
As seaweeds become
covered by the tide they
are supported by the
water and spring back
to life. The sunlight
streams through the
shallow waters allowing
them to photosynthesise.
Photo Vicki Howe (MNR)

Below: **Male Cuckoo
Wrasse (Labrus mixtus)**
Cuckoo Wrasse are
protogynous
hermaphrodites,
meaning they are all
born as females but can
become males when a
dominant male
disappears.
Photo Blaise Bullimore
(MNR)

Left: **Jewel Anemone**
(*Corynactis viridis*)
These underwater
jewels are only a
centimetre wide but will
form large sheets of
thousands of individuals.
There are many colour
varieties, including this
'rhubarb and custard'
combination. They
reproduce by cloning,
with parent anemones
splitting in two.
Photo Kate Lock (MNR)

Right: **The Lucy**

The Dutch coaster *The Lucy* ran aground in Jack Sound on 14th February 1967. It then re-floated and drifted just outside North Haven where it sank in 40 metres of water. The wreck is rich in marine life; Ghost Anemones *(Metridium senile)* and Elegant Anemones *(Sagartia elegans)* smother the mast and ladder.

Photo Blaise Bullimore (MNR)

49

Skomer's Puffin population is the largest in southern Britain with over 6000 pairs returning to breed annually between late March and the end of July.

Puffin (Fratercula artica)
The Puffin's design is a trade off between flight and diving underwater. Like other auks their bones are heavier than most birds, enabling them to dive to depths of 60 metres.
Photo David Miller

Fast and exuberant, the spectacular display of dolphins is a rare but magical sight; leaping and swerving like hooked needles sewing their way through the water.

Above: **Common Dolphins** *(Delphinus delphis)*
While porpoises are seen frequently around the coast dolphins are more elusive and generally remain further out to sea. However, in recent years, pods of up to 300 Common Dolphins have been recorded in St. Brides Bay on several occasions during the summer months.
Photos Lyndon Lomax

Tankers in the Storm Clouds Beyond the Marine Nature Reserve St. Brides Bay is a holding ground for oil tankers from around the world, waiting to load or offload their cargos at the refineries of Milford Haven.
Photo Amber Rowlands

Landscape

Skomer's rock is about 440 million years old and would have been cut off from the mainland by rising sea levels after the last Ice Age. It is essentially volcanic, supporting huge populations of seabirds on cliffs that stand 60 metres high in some places. A deep soil cap over the top of the island provides the perfect habitat for the thousands upon thousands of ground-nesting seabirds that return each year to breed.

Right: **Looking East to Welsh Way from The Neck** Pillows of Thrift bind the fragile terrain above Castle Bay, left to the Rabbits after the ground-nesting seabirds have gone. Photo Jane Matthews

Left: **Thrift** *(Armeria maritima)*, **Wick Basin**
Above: **The Wick**
Flowering Thrift, or Sea Pink, explodes like mini fireworks around Skomer's coast in spring and seabirds return to swarm the rocky shores. Photos Dave Boyle

A human presence on the island dates back between two and five thousand years when the population may have numbered up to 200. Walled fields and settlement remains mark this ancient restructuring of the landscape, but arguably Man's most significant impact was the introduction of the Rabbit in the fourteenth century. Brought to the island to farm for food and fur the Rabbits remained long after their economic importance dwindled and today the island is landscaped by the 10,000 or so now running wild. Their grazing pressure has shaped the island's flora particularly by promoting the Bracken, which in turn provides cover for the Bluebell that normally grows in shady woodland. Their burrows provide convenient ready-made homes for the Puffins and shearwaters.

In 2005 a major rebuilding project started on the island to create improved accommodation and visitor services. Work was structured around the breeding season of the birds to avoid disturbance and in October the Warden's House, which had perched amongst the Puffins at North Haven for nearly fifty years, was flattened to make way for a new, improved facility.

Far left: **Approaching The Amos at Dawn**
Left: **Sea Campion (Silene uniflora)**
In spring the island's coastal banks turn white as the sweet-scented Sea Campion blooms. Great swathes of flowers quiver in the whipping wind.
Photos Jane Matthews, Richard Brown

Right: **Bracken (Pteridium aquilinum)**
Bracken smothers the island in summer. The leaves and shoots, poisonous to Rabbits, are eaten by the unique Skomer Vole.
Photo Tim Guilford

Above left: **Puffin Feeding Chick Below Ground**
Middle: **Puffin Landing**
Left: **Kittiwake (Rissa tridactyla)**
Above right: **The Wick**
Photos Mike Alexander, Brian Hewitt, Dave Boyle, Chris Perrins

Kittiwakes, like other gulls, may lay a clutch of up to three eggs, but Puffins (along with the other auks, shearwaters and petrels) only lay one. With this slow reproduction rate over a long-life span the Puffin must provide a constant supply of fresh fish for its single investment.

Whether below ground or on the cliff ledges Skomer's landscape functions as one huge **breeding platform** for the many species of seabird that return year on year.

Birds are not the only ones to enjoy this **unique offshore environment** and man has an integral part to play in its future.

Left: **Sea Watching**
Skomer attracts up to
15,000 visitors a year.
However, the
overwhelming sense of
space remains and it is
easy to lose the crowd.
Photo Jeff Morgan

Above: **New Base**
The original Warden's
House was built with
the help of the RAF in
1959 and presided over
North Haven for 46
years. An updated
building of the same
footprint was completed
in spring 2007.
Photo Richard Brown

Above: **Demolition of the Warden's House**
Photos Juan Brown, Jane Matthews

Above right: **New accommodation**
Seven wardens made the old gas-lit house their home during its lifespan. In 2005, after weathering a thousand gales, the house was clawed to matchwood in a matter of minutes as part of a £3.1 million Heritage Lottery-funded project.
Photo Jane Matthews

The new improved building boasts solar and wind-powered systems providing hot water and electricity.

The practicalities of farming the island were complicated enough but it was the harsh winter of 1946-47 that spelled the end for Reuben Codd. After a disastrous potato season the economics of farm life became unrealistic and the island was sold to the Nature Conservancy in 1958.

Above: **The Old Farm before Renovations**
Right: **Renovations at The Old Farm**
The original farm house at the centre of the island is thought to have been built around 1700, and the outbuildings were added much later. A loft running the length of the large barn housed the farm workers with horses stabled below. The newly renovated building provides accommodation for researchers and up to 15 paying guests. The gable end staircase leads to a new system of dry-composting toilets, greatly reducing the demand on the island's water supply.
Photos Andy Davies, Jane Matthews

Above left: **Bluebells
(Hyacinthoides
non-scripta)**
In May the island is
awash with a quivering
haze of purple. Bluebells
are a possible relic of
previous woodland cover,
but today Bracken
provides a surrogate
canopy as it grows up
later in the season.
Photo Jane Matthews

Left: **Iron Age Roundhouse** Located near The Wick this human dwelling is thought to date from the early Iron Age. Water would have been collected from South Stream nearby and the surrounding land used for rough grazing and fuel. The remains of what are thought to be ovens or food stores are built into field boundaries nearby.
Photo Jane Matthews

Above: **South Stream Cliff** Layers of volcanic rock provide ledges for a host of seabirds.
Photo Dave Boyle

Castle Bay, Looking East Over Skomer's volcanic base a deep soil cap provides the ideal habitat for burrow-nesting seabirds.
Photo Jane Matthews

The island is landscaped, and its flora shaped, by the Rabbits that have populated Skomer since their introduction in the fourteenth century.

Left: **Welsh Way and South Haven** During spring great smudges of pink and purple transform the island, as Red Campion and Bluebells come into flower. Sea Campion adds a frosting of white around the coastal slopes.
Photo Andy Davies

Below: **Rabbit** *(Oryctolagus cuniculus)* The vegetation on the island is shaped by the grazing Rabbits. An outbreak of Myxomatosis caused a population crash in late 2006 but was followed by exceptional display of flowering plants in 2007.
Photo Dave Boyle

Above: **The Wick**
Left: **Razorbill with Egg**
Right: **Puffins**
Each species has its
own niche on this
spectacular cliff face;
Kittiwakes and
Guillemots on the lower
ledges, Razorbills above
and the Fulmars
towards the top in the
grassier nooks and
crannies. Puffins nest
in burrows on the cliff
tops.
Photos Alison Hayes,
Dave Boyle, Dave Boyle

Arguably the most **impressive cliff** on Skomer, The Wick's basalt ledges and earthy cap support a bustling seabird city.

Populations

Day and night throughout the summer months the island is host to a riotous carnival of breeding seabirds; nearly 20,000 Guillemots, 5,000 Razorbills, more than 10,000 Puffins and 128,000 pairs of Manx Shearwaters. A fragile network of tunnels extends deep into the island's crust, at the end of each a cosy hole shields a Puffin, shearwater (or a family of Rabbits) from hungry gulls above.

Right: **Congregating Puffins at South Haven**
During the breeding season huge crowds of Puffins congregate on the cliff tops at dusk. Communication with neighbours is important and such gatherings are busy with birds head-jerking, bill-tapping and groaning.
Photo Dave Boyle

Guillemots on the cliffs pack tightly together like skittles on to every ledge and crevice, each pair with a single egg between them balanced precariously on warm toes. All these seabirds can live for many years and return to land, after months at sea, to breed. Other, rarer species are also found amid the breeding mayhem. The Skomer Vole, a sub-species of the mainland Bank Vole, thrives on the island's Bracken but is hunted by the Short-eared Owl, gliding low across the valleys. Peregrine, Chough and Curlew are all resident throughout the year.

As the summer ends and the seabirds leave, the island's Grey Seal population takes the spotlight. Between August and December up to 200 pups are born in caves and on beaches around the island. Like seabirds, the seals generally breed each year and can live well into their thirties.

All these populations are scrupulously monitored by the human population - a core of two or three who are joined by volunteers, researchers and visitors throughout the summer months as the island reaches the peak of activity. By late autumn however, as weather fronts shift and the Bracken dies back, Skomer is left to regain its solitary presence once more.

Left: **Grey Seal**
(Halichoreus grypus) – Pup
Grey Seal pups usually weigh about 14kg when born and are expected to triple their weight in the first three weeks of life.
Photo Jane Matthews

Grey seals have been recorded diving to 70m and can possibly go deeper, but they usually feed in shallow coastal waters. Adults breed between August and December.

Left: **Grey Seal, Cow and Pup** Until weaned at approximately three weeks old the Grey Seal pup will live solely off its mother's high-fat milk. Feeding herself up before giving birth, the mother lives off her reserves until the pup is weaned, losing weight as quickly as the pup puts it on. She remains close by, feeding her pup several times a day. Photo Jane Matthews

Puffins
Male Puffins generally have slightly longer and deeper bills than females, and in both sexes the grooves on the bill develop as the bird ages. These grooves are thought to be integral to their mating strategies.
Photos Bob Ball,
Dave Boyle,
Jane Matthews

The Puffin, monochrome throughout the winter months, reaches full colour in time for the breeding season with vermillion legs and a distinct arrow-like beak of orange, yellow and blue.

Acrobats, dancers and clockwork clowns star in Skomer's circus of birdlife.

Above and left: **Chough (Pyrrhocorax pyrrhocorax)**
The Chough has broad 'fingered' wings, scarlet legs and bill. Pembrokeshire is one of the strongholds of this distinctive member of the crow family.
Three to four pairs nest on Skomer.
Photos Dave Boyle

Right: **Chick Puffin**
In July young Puffins venture out of their burrows to limber up, before leaving the island under the cloak of darkness at six weeks old.
Photo Brian Hewitt
Below: **Manx Shearwater at Sea**
Photo Lyndon Lomax

Left: **Razorbill**
Above: **Razorbill Chick**
Over 4,000 Razorbills
nest on ledges and in
rocky crevices around
the coast. Each egg
is incubated for
approximately 35 days.
As with the Guillemot,
the Razorbill chick leaps
from the cliff at less
than three weeks old
and is taken out to sea
by its father.
Photos Dave Boyle

Above: **Great Black-backed Gull (Larus marinus)** The largest of the gulls and main predator of seabirds and Rabbits, there were nearly 300 pairs of Great Black-backed Gulls on Skomer in the 1960s. Species control, compounded by an outbreak of botulism, caused a population crash in the 1970s. Numbers have been generally increasing since the mid 1980s and there have been up to 114 pairs in recent years.
Photo Dave Boyle

Left: **Curlew (Numenius arquata)** Skomer is the last refuge for breeding Curlew in Pembrokeshire. Photo Mike Alexander
Right: **Carrion Crow (Corvus corone), Eggs and Chicks** A few pairs of Carrion Crows nest on rocks and in bushes on Skomer, the red-gaped chicks eagerly awaiting their parents returning with food.
Photos Jane Matthews, Juan Brown

Whether it be trilling
skylarks, the silent swoop of
a Short-eared Owl or swarming
Puffins at dusk, **Skomer's
birding spectacle attracts** the
novice and professional alike.

Above: **Day visitors**
Photo Jeff Morgan
Right: **Short-eared Owl
(Asio flammeus)**
Short-eared Owls, which
nest on the island, can
often be seen hunting
over North Valley during
the day.
Photo Brian Hewitt

Above: **Wheeling Puffins
at South Haven**
Throughout the breeding
season thousands of
Puffins whirl around
their colonies at dusk on
what seem like giant
invisible carousels.
Photo Dave Boyle

Above: **Great Black-backed Gull** *(Larus marinus)*
Middle: **Lesser Black-backed Gull** *(Larus fuscus)*
Left: **Herring Gull** *(Larus argentatus)*

The three species of large gull are identified primarily by their back and leg colour. Great Black-backed Gulls are significantly larger than the other two.
Photos Dave Boyle, Chris Perrins, Andy Davies

Below: **Guillemot**
(Uria aalge) Guillemots
have increased
dramatically on Skomer
in recent decades from a
low point of 2,300
individuals in 1970 to
almost 20,000 in 2005.
Photo Dave Boyle
Right: **Peregrine Falcon**
(Falco peregrinus)
Peregrines have
increased nationally
from the low point of
insecticide poisoning in
the 1950s and 1960s.
Skomer now holds about
4 cliff-nesting pairs.
Photo Juan Brown

Above: **Snowmen**
Right: **Skomer Arms**
Above right: **Ian the Chef**
During the rebuilding project between 2005 and 2007 up to 30 builders stayed in temporary accommodation at the Old Farm. Feeding them all was Ian's job! The old volunteer facilities were replaced in 2006.
Photos Juan Brown, Emily Sharp, Jane Matthews

Display

Skomer – above and below water -
is the stage for a kaleidoscopic display
of changing colours and patterns
throughout the year. The breathtaking
carpets of Bluebells that bloom across
the island in May are replaced by
swathes of Red Campion in June.
It's carnival time with no holds barred
as the flora and fauna spring into life
and show off their wares.
Courting Razorbills, black
and white on sun-baked
guano, tip back their heads
to display their most
brilliant golden mouths.

Above left: **Bluebells**
Photos Jane Matthews,
Juan Brown
Left: **Red Campion**
(Silene dioica)
Photos Juan Brown,
Jane Matthews
On both large and small
scales every detail of
Skomer's many features
deserves a closer look.

Puffins in **full breeding regalia parade** on the cliff-tops with neighbours and mates.

Socialising Puffins
Puffins at The Wick are exceptionally tame and can be watched at very close quarters.
Photo Brian Hewitt

Below the waves, rare sea fans, kelp and soft corals waft in the currents of the Gulf Stream and diving seabirds, silvered by thousands of tiny air bubbles, plunge past in search of food.

Far left: **Diving Puffins**
Above: **Spiral Tube Worm** (*Bispira volunicornis*)
Left: **Elegant Anemone** (*Sagartia elegans*)

Specialist adaptations maximise potential for feeding beneath the waves. Puffins can dive to up to 60m in search of fish, while the feathery arms of the Tube Worm waft food down into its central mouth.

Photos David Miller, Philip Newman (MNR), Kate Lock (MNR)

When magical creatures
surface from the depths they
provide a glimpse of another
wilderness, a reminder that
there is so much more that
goes on unseen.

Left: **Grey Seal**
Above: **Common Dolphins**

Marine mammals are resident around the island all year. Porpoises and (occasionally) dolphins can be spotted off the west coast of the island, breaking the surface of the water. Grey Seals haul out at The Garland Stone and on Rye Rocks at low tide, particularly during the breeding and moulting seasons in spring and autumn. Up to 200 seals can also haul out to sleep on North Haven beach at these times.

Photos Mike Alexander, Lyndon Lomax

With butterflies flip-flapping over the Bracken, moths and dragonflies perched below, there are **spectacular displays of colour**, shape and detail at every turn.

Above: **Scarlet Tiger Moth (Callimorpha dominula)**
Above right: **Emperor Moth (Saturnia pavonia)**
Both these day-flying moths occur in small numbers on the island at different times of the year. Moth traps are set regularly to monitor nocturnal species.
Photos Dave Boyle

Right: **Migrant Hawker (Aeshna mixta)**
Migrating dragonflies appear in small but regular numbers throughout August and September.
Photo Dave Boyle

This dainty and elusive moth feeds on flowering Thrift, and is seen only on the calmest of warm summer days. An artificial pheromone, however, can tempt it into a frenzied mating display.

Left: **Thrift Clearwing**
(Bembecia
muscaeformis)
Above: **Flowering Thrift**
Photos Dave Boyle

Left: **Feather Star
(*Antedon bifida*) and
Painted Top Shell
(*Callistoma zizyphinum*)**
Feather Stars are from
the same group of
animals as the starfish
called the Echinoderms.
They have 10 feather-
like arms with side
branches that are used
to hang onto the rock.
The arms are used
to filter food from
the water and then
transferred down a
groove to the central
mouth.
Photo Kate Lock (MNR)

Above: **The Old Farm**
In Skomer's maritime
climate snow is a rare
phenomenon.
Photo Mike Alexander
Right: **Autumn at
The Wick**
Far right: **North Haven**
Photos Jane Matthews

As the days shorten towards autumn Skomer's fields of Bracken die back, transforming the island into a fiery tangle of copper. Colourful seabirds are long gone but the ever-changing weather maintains the kaleidoscopic scene.

Beauty is not just confined to
open vistas and the conventional
elements of wildlife on Skomer.
It can be found and appreciated
in all things, dead and alive.

Right: **Barn Owl**
(Tyto alba), Feather
In 2004 a pair of
Barn Owls nested in the
workshop at the Old
Farm and successfully
reared two young.
This was first breeding
record for the species
on Skomer since the
late nineteenth century.
Photo Richard Brown

Routine

Skomer is a well-established outpost of ecological study and surveillance with longstanding links to Oxford and Sheffield Universities. Researchers spend up to four months on the island each season building an accurate picture of the health and prosperity of each individual species and the island as a whole.

Left: **Gull Count**
Counting tens of thousands of seabirds can be a daunting task. Here, the Lesser Black-backed Gull nests are about to be marked with canes.
Photo Emily Sharp

A Voluntary Warden scheme provides the facility for up to six people to stay on the island for a week at a time. Their help is central to the running of the reserve and duties include monitoring, path clearing, general maintenance and visitor management. It is a perfect way to experience the island, its wildlife and the magic of being one of the few to remain after the last boat load of visitors has left at the end of the day.

Above left: **Chick Ringing** A study plot of Manx Shearwater burrows is monitored annually which helps determine the longevity and breeding success of the species. Each chick is given a uniquely coded leg ring for re-identification in the future. It will be expected to return to the same area to nest when it reaches breeding age, at about six years old.

Above: **Manx Shearwater chick** In a warm burrow a Manx Shearwater egg will be incubated by each of its parents in turn, for approximately 51 days. Once hatched the chick will continue to live below ground for about a further 69 days during which time it can grow to be twice the weight of an adult. These fat reserves will be essential to the bird's survival after fledging, on its first migratory passage to South America.
Photos Juan Brown

While **nature** is generally left to take its course, data are collected from every imaginable corner of the island.

Left: **South Haven and The Neck** The Neck remains off limits to the general public, only accessed when necessary by staff and researchers for monitoring purposes. This offers a control by which to gauge the human impact on the rest of the island.
Photo Bob Ball

Below: **Double Cliff Shore Monitoring** Double Cliff is the steepest of the shores studied in the Skomer MNR shore monitoring programme. The challenge is to collect the data and take photos of the sample areas by suspending quadrats from a rope attached to pitons whilst floating in a boat – a task only attempted in very calm conditions.
Photo Mark Burton (MNR)

Seabird species are fastidiously monitored each year, forming an invaluable picture of the health of the wider marine environment. With pressures on our seas from commercial fishing and climate change such monitoring is becoming increasingly important.

Left: **The Amos**
Right: **Ringed Guillemot**
As part of a long term
productivity and
survivorship study
Sheffield University
employs a Field
Assistant to stare
through a telescope at
the legs of Guillemots
for four months a year,
predominantly at one
colony on the west coast
of the island. Three
hundred new birds are
ringed each year and
there are a more than
7000 possible birds to
re-identify. This bird was
ringed in 2001.
Photos Dave Boyle

Above: **Volunteers** Much of the work on Skomer relies on the input of Voluntary Wardens, who come from every conceivable niche of society. Each year approximately 50% are newcomers while others return again and again. Of these many veterans Dr. Bill Dixon (right) first volunteered in 1968.

Left: **Haul-out at Matthew's Wick**

Right: **Marked Seal Pup** For over 25 years a census of the Grey Seal breeding population has been carried out, recording as many as 180 pups born per season, scattered over the many remote coves and beaches of the island. Pups are given a colour-coded spray mark at the base of their backs so their progress can be monitored from afar until they shed their first coat at about three weeks old.
Photos Jane Matthews

Above: **Geolocator**
Pioneering research is underway using minuscule tracking devices, small enough to be carried by Manx Shearwaters.
If successful this will give the first detailed data on their yearly migration routes to and from South America.

The device works by recording time of sunrise and day length, from which the bird's position on the globe can be determined.
Photo Dave Boyle

Above right: **Warden's Introductory Talk**
Above left: **Cliff Counts**
The job of the island's staff is to manage the habitat, monitor its species and provide a safe and informed experience for the visitor. Each boat that lands is welcomed with an introductory talk.

Photos Jeff Morgan, Anna Mullarkey

Protection, understanding and education are fundamental to the success of the Reserve.

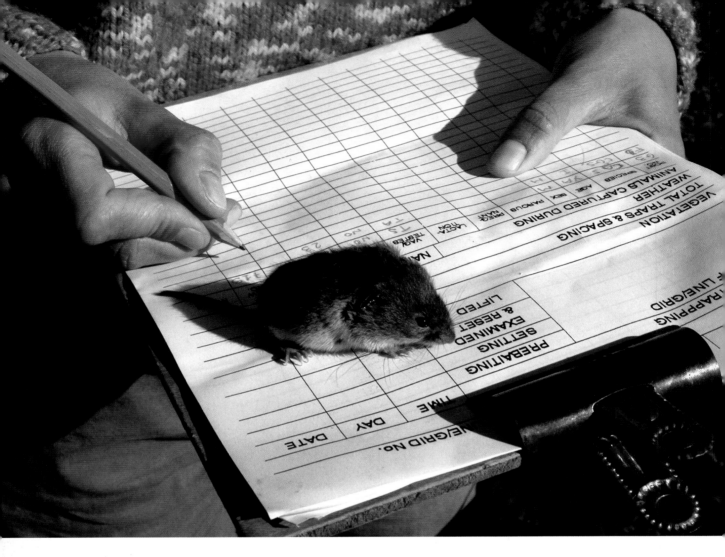

All creatures, resident or visiting, make their mark on Skomer's history in so many different ways. This is what makes it such a fascinating place to be.

Above: **Island Vole Census** The Skomer Vole (*Clethrionomys glareolus skomerensis*) is a subspecies of the Bank Vole unique to the island. Every 10 years a whole island survey is carried out to determine the island's population. In 2005 it was estimated to be between 4 and 10,000, a drop from over 20,000 in the previous decade.
Photo Tim Healing

Above: **Tim Healing**
Tim Healing has been returning to Skomer for over 35 years to monitor the vole population. The skills and equipment needed for his day job as a humanitarian aid worker in some of the most challenging countries on earth often come in handy on the island and he is famous for his breathtaking array of small gadgets.
Photo Juan Brown

Right: **Jean Betteridge (1927-2007)** There is no upper age limit for volunteering on Skomer. Jean first came to the island in her late seventies.
Photo Juan Brown

Busy with day visitors six days a week leaves only Monday, when the island is closed, for essential maintenance, monitoring and a spot of relaxation.

Below: **Cricket** It's not all hard work on a National Nature Reserve! A tradition of inter-island cricket matches has grown over the years, including one against the monks of nearby Caldey Island. In 2005, with a team as smooth as its wicket, Skomer residents fought a noble (but losing) battle against a mainland team.
Photo Jane Matthews

Right: **Visitors leaving the Island** For staff and volunteers many of the duties revolve around the day visitors, their safety and ensuring that all who come onto the island make it off on the boat at the end of the day.
Photo Jeff Morgan

On Skomer there's no such thing as a 9 to 5. Away from the social structures that punctuate life on the mainland, island time is defined largely by seasons and the setting sun.

Left: **Evening over North Valley**

Above: **Fishing for Dinner** Nothing can quite match the taste of fresh mackerel at the end of a hard day. Photos Jane Matthews

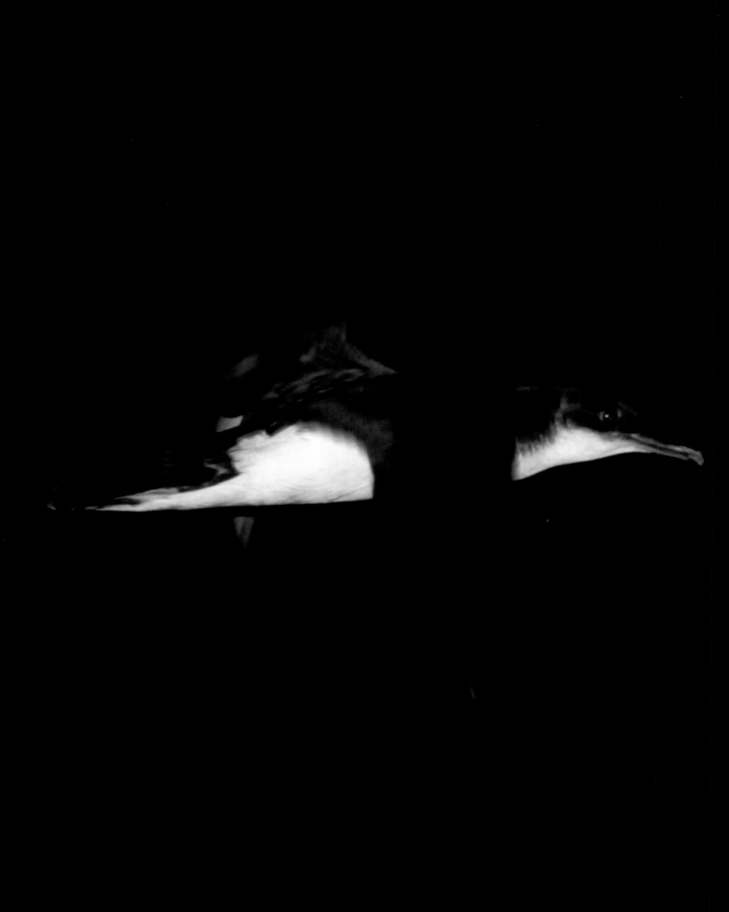

Nightlife

As night falls and streets across the mainland flicker with the glow of television, the sky above Skomer starts to flutter and whirr with the return of the Manx Shearwater.

Page 134/135 and above:
Manx Shearwater
Photos Brian Hewitt
Left: **Moonlit Bluebells**
Photo Flora Moody
The Manx Shearwater relies on complete darkness for its return to land to avoid predation by the Great Black-backed Gull. Moonlit nights spell danger; if they must return to the burrow they do so as swiftly and quietly as possible.

Skomer has the largest single colony of Manx Shearwaters anywhere in the world. These birds fly over seven thousand miles on their migratory passage to South America and find their way back each year to this tiny tip of Wales to breed.

Built for a life at sea with legs set far back on its body, the shearwater is unable to move on land with either grace or precision. It returns to land only in complete darkness to avoid falling prey to the Great Black-backed Gull.

Indoors another Skomer ritual begins... Bird Log has taken place almost nightly throughout the seasons since 1960. All the island's residents convene to record by hand all the day's sightings. Although virtually un-photographed, Bird Log's testimony lies in the volumes of data that now exist forming an invaluable record of seasonal and long-term changes in numbers of birds and other wildlife.

During the day shearwaters that are not on eggs feed far out to sea. At dusk they raft in huge numbers waiting to return to land after dark.

Left: **Manx Shearwaters at Sea** Shearwaters can embark on long distance fishing trips for up to seven days while the partner bird remains below ground. Recent tagging has shown, contrary to previous belief, that feeding birds head north into the Irish Sea as far as the Mull of Kintyre.
Photo Lyndon Lomax

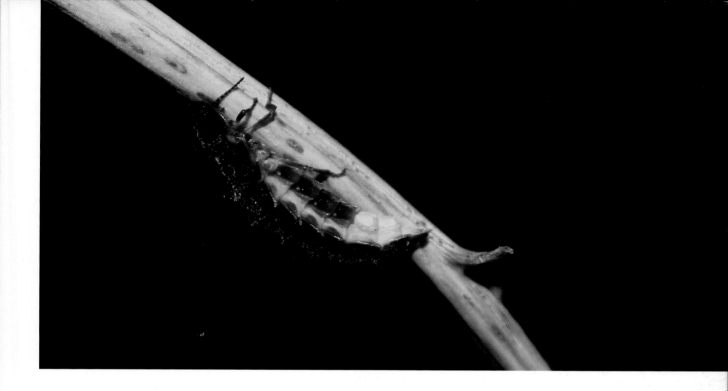

The festival of sound and light continues until just before dawn. With the most dazzling array of costumes, the island's nocturnal species threaten to upstage their daytime counterparts.

Left: **Puffin below Ground** Puffin activity often peaks at dusk, when chicks are below ground, and then again at dawn. But little is known about their activities throughout the night.
Photo Richard Brown

Above: **Glow-worm (Lampyris noctiluca)**
Right: **European Storm Petrel (Hydrobates pelagicus)** Glow-worms often light up the track from North Haven on summer nights. The secretive Storm Petrel breeds in a few remote boulder beaches on the island and, like the shearwaters, only returns at night.
Photos Dave Boyle

Above: **Night Flight**
Right: **Outside its Burrow** The highest concentration of shearwaters is found at North Haven and, on a dark or foggy night, the sky is filled with incoming birds, calling to their partners below ground. Breeders and non-breeders alike litter the banks and the lights of the mainland serve only to remind that it is near, yet very, very far. Photo Jane Matthews, Dave Boyle

Nothing compares to the ghostly sight and sound of the Manx Shearwaters' return. It is the largest colony anywhere in the world and the only easily accessible place in Britain to witness such a spectacle.

Jeremy Grange

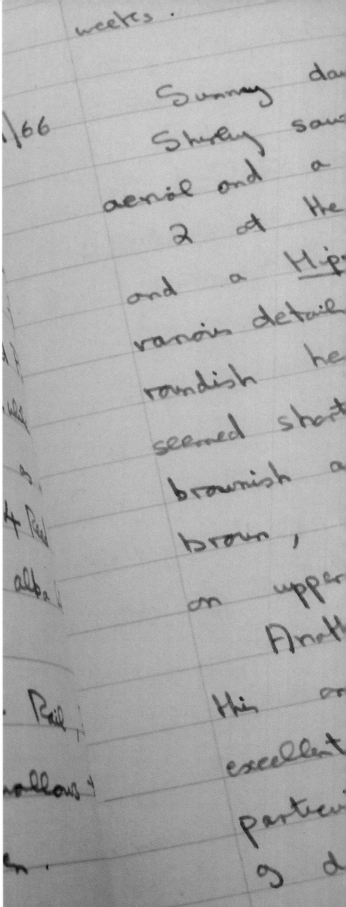

Above and right:
Bird Log
Photos Jane Matthews

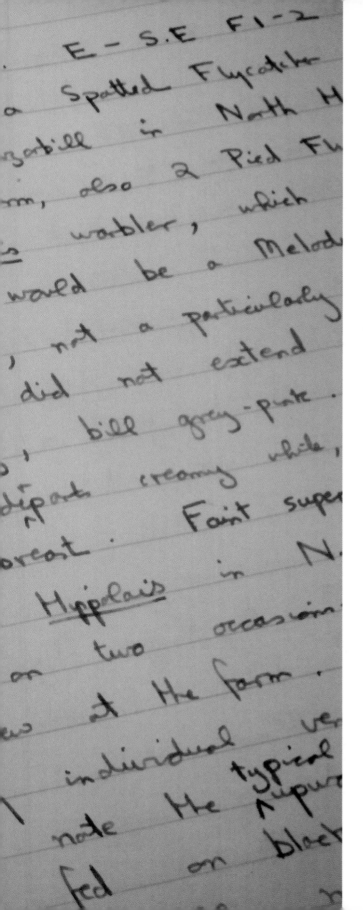

Bird Log

The pencil-point hovers
above the page's horizon,
lifting for a moment from its hunt
as latecomers, breathing apology,
steal in from the twilight's
pendent stillness.

You resume the broken chant
and words take flight:
guillemot and gannet, cormorant, chough.

This nightly vigil embraces
the island. A final roll-call
before sleep, testing the textures
of presence and absence:
travellers, visitors,
fixtures and departures.

In the bubble of light, fed
by the generator's heartbeat,
stories unfold like butterflies:

the migrant, displaced and lost,
a stained glass ornament
pressed against the window;

the cow seal, heaving herself
over rocks to rid the beach of you, your rout
reflected in her pup's gibbous eyes;
a sunfish – monstrous, incomplete –
hove-to and helpless in the sound.
You log each memory with a tick.

As islanders wend their way
back to their beds by torchlight
they dodge shearwaters, frogs
and toads. On a damp night
the paths can be littered with
all three.

Left: **Common Toad
(Bufo bufo)**
Above: **Common Frog
(Rana temporaria)**
Skomer has an
unusually high density
of frogs and toads, and
an especially orange
form of Common Frog.
Both can be seen large
numbers on the tracks
in wet weather.
Photos Richard Brown,
Dave Boyle

Just before dawn the island falls quiet and the night's secrets get hidden away. All that remain are the discarded wings of those that didn't survive; their bodies stripped clean by the gulls.

Left: **Dawn on the West Coast**
Below: **Carcass**
Photos Bob Ball, Emily Sharp

"...the quite smooth sea turned again in its perpetual come and go, and took us slowly back in so many hours, till we found ourselves again by evening where we had started, at the mouth of Jack Sound."
Hilaire Belloc, *The Cruise of the Nona* (1925).

Above: **Skomer from the West**
Left: **South of The Neck**
Photos Jane Matthews

Skomer's Natural History

Juan Brown

440 million years ago, during the Silurian geological period, volcanic activity laid down the sequence of rocks that forms Skomer today. This sequence extends out from the Marloes Peninsula on the mainland to Middleholm, Skomer, Grassholm, and out to the Smalls – a group of islets about 22 km to the west. Erosion of surrounding softer rocks and fault activity isolated these hard rocky outposts, creating islands, the biggest and most accessible of which is Skomer.

The characteristic, relatively flat-topped 'tableland' was created by marine activity when Skomer was underwater between 80 and 90 million years ago. Upon this, a deep soil cap has formed which provides sanctuary for the burrow-nesting Puffin and Manx Shearwater. The surrounding sea forms a barrier to land predators. Skomer is the biggest Puffin colony in southern Britain (more than 10,000 birds) while the 128,000 pairs of Manx Shearwater represent one third of the entire world population. This species is particular about where it nests, requiring soil in which to burrow, a lack of land predators, access to rich feeding grounds, and enough darkness to allow a safe return from a day's fishing (so northern latitudes that stay light during the summer are unsuitable); Skomer fits the bill on all counts.

Above ground a thick vegetation has developed. In mid-late May Bluebells form dense tracts. This species has a global distribution limited to the Atlantic coast of Europe. As the Bluebells wither in June, Bracken takes over, forming a shady canopy akin to the woodland that Bluebells are normally associated with. Amongst the vegetation nests a large colony of Lesser Black-backed Gulls, forming a significant percentage of the world's population of the race *graelsii*.

The vertical igneous cliffs on the edge of this island plateau provide safe inaccessible ledges for other nesting seabirds: the Kittiwake, a strictly-marine gull which sticks a cup of mud and grass to the rock in which to lay its eggs; Guillemot – a penguin-like bird which does not even bother to build a nest, laying a single cone-shaped egg on bare rock, huddled together with thousands of its own; and Razorbill, present on Skomer in internationally important numbers.

Skomer provides a haven for Grey Seals – present all year and pupping in the autumn – while its isolation has resulted in the evolution of its own race of Bank Vole, the unique Skomer Vole.

Having been legally protected for over 40 years, Skomer hosts a wealth of wildlife, its relative accessibility has enabled conservationists, scientists and the general public to study and enjoy this national treasure without compromising the flora and fauna which make it so special.

Designations at a glance:
- National Nature Reserve
- Site of Special Scientific Interest
- Marine Nature Reserve
- Special Protection Area (European)
- Scheduled Ancient Monument
- Geological Conservation Review site
- Within Pembrokeshire Islands Special Area of Conservation (European)
- Within Pembrokeshire Coast National Park
- Part of Heritage Coast

Contributors

Jane Matthews
Jane Matthews was born in Bristol, studied Fine Art at Oxford University and Art History at The Courtauld Institute in London. She was working as an artist in the television and film industry in London when she first went to Skomer, as a volunteer. She now lives on the island with Juan - the warden, their daughter Martha and about half a million seabirds. She paints, writes, takes photographs, studies the Grey Seal breeding season and rarely misses London.

Iolo Williams
Iolo Williams was born and brought up in mid Wales, and having studied for a degree in ecology in London, returned to Wales to work for the RSPB. He spent nearly 15 years as Species Officer for Wales, working on a wide range of different birds, including Black Grouse, Hen Harrier, Red Kite, Chough and Lapwing. He left the organisation in 1998 to work full-time in the media and he now works mainly for BBC Wales, with the odd foray into Radio 4. As well as broadcasting, Iolo has written several books on wildlife in both Welsh and English. He is a keen sportsman, is married to Ceri and has two young boys, Dewi and Tomos.

Matthew Parris
Matthew Parris, who was born and educated in South Africa, Cyprus, Rhodesia and Swaziland, has been a civil servant, an MP, a television presenter and (for many years now) a Times journalist and radio broadcaster. He has led expeditions to the Sahara, South America and the Andes, spent the winter of 2000 on Kerguelen (Desolation Island) in the Southern Ocean, among albatross, penguins and elephant seals, and most recently (for BBC Radio 4) followed camel trains from the highlands of Ethiopia into the inferno of the Danakil depression on their ancient route to collect salt. He visited Skomer while making a radio series about animal migration.

David Miller
Born in Lancashire in 1966, David Miller now lives and works in the heart of the west Wales countryside, in a wooded valley near the Taf and Towy estuaries with the dramatic Pembrokeshire coastline on his doorstep. He paints mostly British wildlife, usually in oils, travelling widely to gather reference and inspiration for his work.
www.davidmillerart.co.uk

Brian Hewitt
From an early age I have had a deep interest in wildlife and, later on, photography. With a welcome career change, I am now lucky enough to be able to combine them both, full-time. Skomer is one of those special places that gets its hooks in to you. If I'd known about the volunteering I think I would have done it a long time ago.
www.brianhewittimages.co.uk

Lyndon Lomax
After 30 years with British Gas, based in the Midlands, the move to Pembrokeshire was made in 1997. Since then visiting the Islands, the cliff tops, and off shore boat trips have been almost a daily occurrence both to study and enjoy the marine life available to us. If my enthusiasm and some of my pictures excite others to

enjoy the wonders of our coastal birds and marine life then my time here will have been more than well spent.

Jeff Morgan
Jeff is a Wales-based photojournalist who works regularly for *The Guardian* and the national press. His shots have appeared in publications worldwide.

Juan Brown
Juan Brown has lived and worked on islands for over 10 years. He was a warden on Noss in Shetland and the Farne Islands in Northumberland prior to becoming the Warden of Skomer in 1999. He is a keen naturalist with a particular interest in birds.

Jeremy Grange
Jeremy Grange lives in North Wales and works for the BBC as a radio producer. He has visited Skomer on several occasions and 'Bird Log' was inspired by a night on the island recording a programme about Manx Shearwaters. The poem won BBC Wildlife Magazine's Poet of the Year Competition 2005.

Emily Sharp
My first Skomer experience was as a volunteer five years ago and I've been coming to take photographs of the island ever since. I'm usually to be found in London, working in a busy drug and alcohol treatment centre or singing classical music. What I most love about Skomer is its wild, magical landscape, bird log and falling asleep to the deathly cries of the Manx Shearwaters.

Bob Ball
I first volunteered on Skomer in 1995 and like many others I was soon hooked. Once or twice a year I leave the lovely Surrey Hills and the Highways Agency behind for a week in another world; nature at its finest with the glorious Pembrokeshire coast as its backdrop. It's a photographer's dream island. The biggest thrill is introducing family and friends to the island.

Dave Boyle
Dave Boyle has been studying Skomer's seabird populations as part of a longstanding study by the Edward Grey Institute at Oxford University. Between seasons on Skomer he has worked on eradicating rats from Canna Island in the Hebrides and cats from Ascension Island in the mid-Atlantic. He is also a qualified cabinet-maker and bus driver.

Chris Perrins
Professor at Oxford University and eminent ornithologist, Chris Perrins has been supervising the research work of the Edward Grey Institute of Ornithology on Skomer for over 30 years.

Tim Healing
Tim Healing is a humanitarian aid worker who spends a lot of time abroad in some rather dodgy places. He did his PhD on Skomer voles starting in 1970 and now visits the island annually as part of a long term study of the voles. He says it keeps him (fairly) sane.

Mike Alexander
Mike Alexander's passion for conservation began as a 13 year old boy when he was taken on a day trip to Skomer. He worked on various reserves until, eventually, he became Warden of Skomer in 1976. The ten years he spent on the island confirmed everything he had ever believed about the importance of nature conservation. In 1991 he became Conservation Management Coordinator for the Countryside Council for Wales, with a key responsibility for the management of all the National Nature Reserves in Wales.

Amber Rowlands

Amber is a professional freelance photographer based in London, whose work spans portraiture and landscape. Along with sister Jessie she was first introduced to Skomer as a volunteer several years ago by their stepfather. Neither knew what to expect, having never done volunteering work before. It was an incredible experience for both of them and life changing for Jessie. "Being able to stay and be a part of the island is a great privilege." www.amber-rowlands.com

MNR

The Skomer Marine Nature Reserve is managed by the Countryside Council for Wales. The photos are a collection by the MNR team and long term volunteers; Phil Newman, Kate Lock, Blaise Bullimore, Rob Gibbs, Mark Burton, Vicki Howe, Rohan Holt.

Alison Hayes (left)

Alison Hayes is a visual artist specialising in photographic and video/sound installation artworks. She hopes to inspire new ideas and directions in the course of wildlife preservation and how people perceive art through her new body of artwork based on and around Skomer and Grassholm Islands.

Flora Moody (right)

Flora Moody is a professional photographer and acting as an assistant at times on this project.

Additional photographs by **Roscoe Howells**, **Tim Guilford** and **Anna Mullarkey**.

Richard Brown

Richard Brown became Assistant Warden on Skomer in 2005, since when he has been lucky enough to work alongside many of the other contributors. Previously he was a Pink Pigeon Researcher in Mauritius, a Reserve Warden in his native North Yorkshire, a BTO Yellow Wagtail Researcher and a burger factory employee. He now calls Skomer home.

Andrew Davies

Andrew specialises in landscape, wildlife and environmental photography. Since moving to Pembrokeshire in 1999 he has developed an interest in coastal and marine wildlife subjects and works in web design for educational and conservation organisations.

Index